Axolotl Facts for Kids

*Explore the Fascinating World of
Axolotls and Learn Everything You
Need to Know about Them*

Table of Contents

Introduction

Have you ever come across an Axolotl? Has that name ever been mentioned to you before? You probably haven't heard of it since these magnificent and mysterious creatures don't get as much attention as they deserve.

"Axolotl" (which is pronounced *Ax-oh-lot-ul)* is commonly referred to by Australians and New Zealanders as the Mexican walking fish. However, this is not entirely accurate since they're not fish at all. They're actually amphibians — nocturnal salamanders, to be precise. These tiny, fascinating beings are the inspiration behind a lot of today's comic books, cartoons, and motion pictures. Think of your favorite superhero, like Wolverine, from the X-Men. He had the ability to regenerate his tissue when injured, making him nearly indestructible, just like these beautiful amphibians can do. This specific feature is one of many that left a lot of scientists in awe, wondering how this small being developed this incredible ability to restore itself after harm.

Despite their ability to regenerate and heal themselves when injured, they are among some of the critically endangered species in the world. This makes learning about them all the more important to help protect their existence.

This breed of salamander defies the rules of biology, such as metamorphosis. This process is the natural change that happens to all living beings after they are born. This change is usually physical, like when a butterfly emerges from its cocoon or a frog from its egg. This little guy maintains features acquired from birth throughout the rest of its life, such as its webbed feet. So, in simpler terms, they keep their baby-like appearance throughout their entire life.

As you go through this book, you'll get a closer look at what exactly an Axolotl is, such as their defining features, how they live, and how they behave. You'll learn about their strengths and if they are safe to be around and keep as a pet.

Chapter 1: What Is an Axolotl?

It's unlikely that your mind can fathom the magical myth behind the Axolotl when you first see it. As legend has it, this Mexican amphibian is closely linked to the god, Xolotl, which was an ancient Aztec god that was focused on escaping his own sacrifice. In Mexican culture, this creature is revered as the embodiment of defying death. In Nahuatl, which is informally known as the Aztec language, the letters *"atl"* mean water, and *"xolotl"* means monster. Put them together, and you get an aquatic monster (or water monster). In other translations, you may hear it being referred to as the water dog. There are people who pronounce it as *"aksolotol"* or *"asholotol."* The Spanish word for axolotl is *"ajolote"*; however, this term is used loosely in Mexico to describe all salamanders.

1. Xolotl, an ancient Aztec god. Source:
https://commons.wikimedia.org/wiki/File:Xolotl_1.jpg

The story states that in order to escape his own execution, the god, Xolotl, changed form into a corn plant with two stalks. When he was discovered by the executioner, he fled again, changing into a double maguey plant. When he was discovered again, he made one last transformation into an axolotl and hid in the water, where the executioner finally came upon him and killed him. This may seem like a sad end to the little creature; however, if you look at the broader picture, the story has a deeper meaning. The little salamander represents perseverance, resilience, the ability to cope with change, and a very strong will to fight and survive.

In other tales, it is said that Xolotl was transformed into a salamander and sentenced to live as a water-dwelling monster for eternity in the darkness.

What Is an Axolotl?

The Axolotl is a Mexican amphibian that represents the god Xolotl (the god of fire and lightning) in the ancient Aztec culture. Their scientific name is Ambystoma mexicanum. While some describe it as ugly, this creature has many other redeeming features that mask its unusual appearance.

2. An Axolotl is a Mexican amphibian that represents the god, Xolotl. Source: https://www.pexels.com/photo/white-fish-under-water-2168831/

They are most likely found in one specific location on earth, in the fresh water of Lake Xochimilco and Chalco, as well as in the canals and waterways surrounding them. The lake is situated near Mexico City, in Central America.

What Does It Look Like?

Axolotls are quite small — they come in many colors and resemble an overgrown tadpole with widely-spaced eyes. The eyes are round and dark, with yellow luminous irises. Their average life span is 10 to 15 years. The average size of an Axolotl is around 20 to 25 centimeters long (about 9 inches), and they weigh between 2.11 and 8 ounces. This is the size of a standard envelope or a fully-grown guinea pig. They have a lizard-like body. They also have small legs and feet, which, interestingly enough, they aren't born with but rather grow them a few weeks later. They are part of the salamander family (Mole Salamanders); however, as they grow, they don't lose their gills and cannot live on land like their cousins. Their natural habitat is water, and they tend to keep their wispy gills, which are basically their trade mark.

Their gills are really hard to miss as they grow on the outside of their body in the form of feathery appendages. You can imagine how cute that makes them look.

In addition to the gills, they tend to have a fin that extends from the back of their head to the tip of their tail.

Their colors range from brown and gray to pink and green, often with specs of gold or olive colors. Nonetheless, albino, leucistic, pink, and white are the most prevalent hues while breeding in captivity. Their long tail comes in handy when they're swimming, and they have little webbed feet. A common feature that people notice about them is that they always look like they're smiling because of the shape of their mouths. Their mouth stays open for a few seconds after they swallow their meal, which is one of the main reasons they appear to be smiling. So, if you think they're happy to see you, think again... they're just eating.

They have a feature that closely resembles an iguana, which is the ability to camouflage and hide in plain sight. They use this little trick to hide themselves from both predators and prey alike. This trait is common among several members of the salamander family. Even though they mainly use their gills to breathe, Axolotls also develop lungs, which they use to breathe on the water's surface.

The Unique Features of These Remarkable Creatures

A lot is still unknown about these creatures, such as the reason for the change in color between the wild dwellers and those bred in captivity and their remarkable ability to overcome injuries by using their regenerative talents. However, there are some facts that people have been able to dig up about these salamanders.

They Can Regenerate

A scar forms after the healing process when a human being gets an injury of any kind, like a cut on the arm or a scrape to the knee. This scar is usually a different color and feel from the rest of your skin. If a person loses a limb, such as an arm, a leg, or a finger, that limb does not grow back. However, with Axolotls, the case is quite different. They are literally the superheroes of the animal kingdom. While some crabs can regrow their body parts, axolotls are a bit more advanced than that. They don't just stop at growing back their limbs. They can regrow organs in their fully functioning whole forms and even regrow their own brain.

Another intriguing fact that would be very useful if researchers could replicate it in humans is that axolotls don't reject other body parts. If one axolotl lost a limb and received one from another one of its peers, its body will not reject it like a human body would.

Can They See?

3. Axolotl's don't see very well. Source: Monika Korzeniec, CC BY-SA 3.0 <http://creativecommons.org/licenses/by-sa/3.0/>, via Wikimedia Commons: https://commons.wikimedia.org/wiki/File:6_maja_06_r._ZOO_2 04.jpg

Axolotls don't see very well. However, they have an excellent sense of smell that they rely on when they're out searching for food. They naturally prefer murky areas with less light in order to keep their other senses alert. By doing so, they are able to defend themselves against predators better.

4. Axolotls look like babies. Source: https://pixabay.com/illustrations/baby-axolotl-axolotl-animal-7693810/

These creatures don't go through a growth spurt or change their physical form following their birth. Think of them as Peter Pan... forever young. This process is called neoteny (or paedomorphism). Neoteny (or neotenic) means that they reach puberty without losing their baby-like characteristics (larval features). Scientists have run some tests on these little beings to see if they can trigger a change that would give them more adult-like features. It was determined that when they are injected with a chemical called iodine, the process of metamorphosis starts, and they take on an adult form. Basically, that means they can shed their gills and join their cousins on the mainland.

Their Diet

These amphibians have no teeth. How do they eat, you may ask? Well, they have a rather powerful suction ability that they employ to crush and cram down their prey. This process is called Hoover dining. Their normal prey consists of worms, insect larvae, mollusks, some fish, and crustaceans. This small menu is enough to classify them among the carnivores. They also don't care whether or not what they're eating is dead or alive. They don't let any bite go to waste.

If they are hungry enough, they can turn on their own kin. In some recorded cases, young axolotls have bitten off bits of their siblings and family members.

When raised in captivity, their diet typically consists of fish pellets, earthworms, and slices of beef liver, among other things.

This classification does not make them immune to predators. Birds tend to have a special taste for these tiny salamanders. During the day, they hide themselves among vegetation and mud to avoid becoming dinner to another predator. At night, they emerge hungry and ready to search for their own prey.

They Are Endangered Species

Previously found throughout a series of lakes and wetlands all around central Mexico, these little guys now live within only four square miles of their natural habitat. This is mostly because of pollution, nearby development, and invasive species (like tilapia and carp, which are not native to that specific ecosystem). Because scientists are interested in studying their ability to regenerate and its possible applications in medicine (specifically in healing incurable diseases or regenerating limbs), their survival is ensured when bred in captivity. However, the same cannot be said for those born in the wild. Researchers are using axolotls to try and find ways to regenerate or heal spinal cord injuries, heart and lung disease, jaws, and, in some cases, brain injuries.

In their natural habitat, it is estimated that the total number of these salamanders had been reduced by 90% in 2009. They were considered extinct in 2015 until one was found a week later in the wild.

Environmentalists are trying to raise the water level in Lake Xochimilco to make it more axolotl friendly. These days, it is estimated that there are only about 1,000 axolotls remaining in the wild.

They Have Many Kids and They Like to Dance

Axolotls can breed up to three times in a single year. On average, the female can lay between 100 and 300 eggs each time — sometimes, the number can go up to 1,000 eggs (that's a lot of eggs considering their size). If they are bred in captivity, they can sometimes mate and produce more eggs than they could in the wild. These eggs are laid in the lake or river bed and left until they hatch after two weeks. Once they hatch, their survival is their own responsibility. Their parents don't stick around to protect them or teach them how to stay alive.

When axolotls are six months old, that's when they decide to get married. The adults come together and move around in a circular motion as if they're dancing. This dance resembles the hula dance as they shake their tail and lower body.

5.   Axolotls like to dance. Source:
https://pixabay.com/illustrations/axolote-water-xochimilco-
animals-4465023/

They Are Lone Creatures

These little amphibians are solitary animals. They don't usually travel in groups or pairs. Even though they have one of the most fascinating mating rituals, they usually part ways when they're done. Even though they're not the most social of beings, they can't be outright accused of being unfriendly. This type of behavior is evidence that they are highly intelligent creatures and that they only engage in social activities when needed.

Their Genome Is Uncharacteristically Large

Axolotl genomes are ten times larger than those of humans. With over 32 billion bases in their DNA, decoding their genome has proven to be a formidable task for scientists. Understanding that those few billion DNA bases hold the secret to understanding how these organisms use stem cells for regeneration and healing is crucial. When scientists were able to pinpoint the two primary genes in charge of the capacity for regeneration, progress was achieved. Though it doesn't sound like much, it is still quite impressive, considering the huge pool that they're looking through.

Axolotls as Pets

Can you own an Axolotl as a pet at home? The answer is yes. If you've never owned a pet before, trying something a little easier than an amphibian may be better. You should also consider that because there aren't many of them out there, most vets don't have much information about how to care for them.

6. Axolotl's can be pets. Source: Kyngodev, CC BY-SA 4.0 <https://creativecommons.org/licenses/by-sa/4.0>, via Wikimedia Commons: https://commons.wikimedia.org/wiki/File:Axolotl_happy.jpg

Even though they have remarkable regenerative and healing abilities, they can still be susceptible to infections and disease from negligence or insufficient care.

Axolotls are not interactive pets, meaning that you can't just pick them up out of the water and manhandle them or play with them.

You also need to make sure that it is legal to keep one in your home. In some states and countries, it is prohibited to own them, like in Maine, California, and Virginia.

You may also require a permit to be able to get one. It is better to get one from a breeder rather than from a pet store, as the former tend to be more informative and engage in ethical practices than the latter.

Are They Poisonous?

No, these cute little creatures do not pose any danger to humans. The only instance where they could be considered dangerous is if they are carrying a disease or an infection that can be transmitted to humans. Otherwise, their skin is poison-free, and humans can touch them safely. However, you need to make sure that you've washed your hands thoroughly and disinfected them before you attempt to touch the amphibian. They may not be poisonous to you, but you could very easily transfer all kinds of bacteria and pollutants from your skin to their outer skin.

What Do They Need?

You'll need to get an aquarium and fill it up with water that is slightly cooler than the room's temperature. You'll also need a water filter and a substrate, and don't go crazy with tank decorations. They tend to thrive in a 20+ gallon enclosure, and because they are lone creatures and territorial, it is best to only keep one.

They don't need as many toys and artifacts within the enclosure due to their super-sensitive skin and the ease with which they can be injured. So, keep them away from sharp objects.

Make sure the temperature of the water remains cool and that you treat it regularly with a water conditioner in order to remove substances like chlorine. This makes the environment safer for their gills and skin. The water should have a pH level of between 6.5 and 7.5.

Your pet axolotl will eat two to three times a week for a period of five to 10 minutes each. The best way to give them food is to drop small portions that are cut up into small pieces into the tank to avoid choking them.

Chapter 2: Axolotl Habitats

Axolotls are such unique creatures that you must wonder where they come from to be so amazing. There are very few axolotls left in the wild, with their population size sitting at less than 1,000. Most of them are found in labs so that specialized scientists can study their incredible abilities, like regenerating their limbs and being more resistant to cancer than most animals, or else they are found in zoos so that this amphibian wonder can be around for generations. Sadly, axolotls can't enjoy their lives in the wild like they once did because humans have interfered with their habitat.

As amphibians, axolotls use their specialized gills on the sides of their face to breathe underwater. They also have lungs so that they can breathe on land. Therefore, they live in swampy marshes where they can move between water and wet soil. They are perfectly adapted to this environment because they blend in with the brown shades surrounding them. Before people interfered with their homes, they were close to the top of the food chain, without any natural predators. Times have changed for the axolotls, who now have to worry about fish predators that humans introduced into their once peaceful homes.

7. *Axolotls use their specialized gills to breathe underwater. Source: https://unsplash.com/photos/a-white-and-black-animal-laying-on-top-of-rocks-2aWsTp5Jt4E?utm_content=creditShareLink&utm_medium=referral&utm_source=unsplash*

The axolotl is a lot younger than many of their salamander cousins, only having been around for about 10,000 years. Compare this to some of the oldest salamander fossils that go all the way back 164 million years. Looking at how axolotls live in the wild can teach people a lot about how amphibians evolve because they are such a new species. That's why it is important to save the habitats of axolotls so that people can understand more about the living world. As people start to see the impacts of pollution, it is becoming clearer that humans have to look at the actions they take and how they affect nature.

Animals are shaped by their environments. Looking at the habitats that axolotls naturally live in can tell you a lot about them. The habitats of these interesting guys teach us about the world and, surprisingly, about people as well. Axolotls, like other salamander species, are amphibians. This means they live on water and on land. Most scientists believe that all life, including humans' ancient ancestors, comes from water.

Studying how amphibians survive on both land and in water shows us how animals that lived in water were able to evolve to start living on land.

Where Do Axolotls Call Home?

The reason why axolotls' numbers have fallen so much in nature is that they are found in extremely specific places, which means that their habitat is rare. Their name hints at where they are from because the name comes from the Aztec culture, which is native to Mexico. Axolotls are named after the ancient god, Xolotl, who is the god of fire and lighting and who shapeshifts into salamanders. Their whisker-like gills give them a godly appearance — something like a dragon. Axolotls are not found all over Mexico but are located in the tiny region of Lake Xochimilco and Lake Chalco in Mexico City.

8.   Axolotls are located in the region of Lake Xochimilco. Source: Hernán García Crespo, CC BY 2.0 <https://creativecommons.org/licenses/by/2.0>, via Wikimedia Commons: https://commons.wikimedia.org/wiki/File:Lake_Xochimilco_in_S outhern_Mexico.jpg

As more people moved into Mexico City and started building roads, factories, and houses, the natural habitat of axolotls became smaller and smaller. The reckless pollution that people brought with them also damaged the lake homes of the axolotls. Naturally, axolotls had very few predators as they were only being eaten by birds of prey occasionally. In the 1970s, carp fish were artificially introduced into their habitat. The carp found the axolotls quite tasty, so snacking on the tiny critters also reduced their numbers.

The Xochimilco-Chalco basin, which the axolotls call home, was about 77 square miles big at one time, but it is fast becoming a lot smaller. The marshy swamplands are perfect for axolotls, which enjoy a warm, wet area to make themselves nice and cozy. Very little is known about how they behave when left to their natural habits because the areas where they live are hard to get to, so scientists don't often get the opportunity to study them in their homes.

Axolotls evolved the incredible superpower of being able to change colors so that they can blend in with their surroundings. Depending on the color of the shallow water you will find them enjoying a swim in, they either become darker or lighter. Sometimes, you see axolotls that are white or pink, but these don't usually survive in the wild, and they have been bred by humans. The axolotls that humans have bred to be brighter will not be able to live in the wild because they will stick out like a sore thumb, making them easy pickings for predators. The brighter colors of axolotls are killed off quickly, which is why the surviving amphibians pass on their dark-colored genes to their young.

Axolotls are small, ranging between 9 and 18 inches. Their size allows them to hide in difficult-to-reach places and makes them even harder to spot when they are camouflaged.

Therefore, researchers are unsure about the exact number of them still found in nature because they can be so difficult to locate. Their hiding skills are one of their best tricks for survival. Their habitat helps them hide because they can slip in between plants when they feel like they are in danger.

As fewer axolotls are found in nature now, they are more prone to developing disease because their selection of suitable mates has been negatively impacted. Most of the axolotls on earth are no longer found in Mexican canals and swamps but are now being kept as pets in homes, and in some countries, they are getting served up on a dinner plate in fancy restaurants. Although human interest in animals is keeping them alive, their quality of life is not as good as it would have been if they were free in an undisturbed habitat. Think about if you were locked up in your room all day and never given some time to go outside and play... you would probably also not feel too great.

Now that most axolotl homes are no longer in Lake Xochimilco, where they belong, it brings up many questions about how humans interfere with nature and what that means for how animals live their daily lives. Instead of swimming freely, axolotls are mostly trapped in enclosures far smaller than the areas where they would be free to explore in the wild. Although breeding axolotls in labs and for pets increases their numbers, it is not the same as if they were able to live in their natural environments. Scientific research into axolotls and how they grow back body parts and fight cancer would be incomplete if they could not be properly studied in their habitats.

Although small canals have been built to grow natural axolotl populations in Lake Xochimilco, if humans keep expanding into their territory and pollution is not reduced, axolotls in the wild will likely go extinct, leaving only those that remain in zoos, pet shops, restaurants, and labs. Most of the water in Lake Chalco has been drained for urban development, meaning that there is not much left for the axolotls.

Axolotls need mud-water and plant life to survive. They burrow into mud and in between plants to hide during the day. They come out in the cover of darkness at night to hunt. They eat different kinds of worms, insect larvae, small fish, and mollusks that are readily available all over their swampy homes. Experts recommend they should be fed this mixed diet when they are kept at home in order to mimic the swamp they come from.

Whether they spend their time ducking and diving in between plants in marshy wetlands or are behind glass for you to admire them in an aquarium, there is no denying that axolotls are wonderful and interesting creatures. Hopefully, how much humans love them and the research scientists need will motivate people to be more responsible with pollution and restore some of their homelands. Maybe sometime in the future, axolotls will be allowed to leave their common zoo and laboratory homes to be reunited with the swampy waters that they love.

The Importance of Their Natural Habitats

The Xochimilco-Chalco basin, the natural home of axolotls, is a tourist attraction that means a lot to many locals due to their ancestors' high regard for the region. Lake Xochimilco has been used for farming for hundreds of years. The basin also provides natural resources to people living around it, like oxygen and water. Mexico is one of the most biodiverse regions in the world, with many plants and animals found in the country that cannot be found anywhere else on the planet. Lake Xochimilco is part of a marshy swamp that once spanned far and wide but has now become a few isolated places that people attempt to conserve.

Wildlife protection groups in Mexico have made efforts to restore some of the damage that has been done by pollution and construction. They have built areas where axolotls can live undisturbed in their natural homes, but their population numbers have not grown much to this day. The Xochimilco-Chalco basin is important because if it is lost, the natural home for many animal and plant species, including the axolotl, would be destroyed.

It is easy to recreate the conditions where axolotls live in a fish tank or an aquarium, so some people do not see why their homes need to be taken care of. The problem with thinking like this is that you do not see the wider ecosystem being messed with in a way that could affect the entire planet. Everything on earth is connected, so changes to sensitive ecosystems could cause a domino effect that would be felt around the world.

9. Axolotls can live in aquariums if the proper conditions are recreated. Source: https://unsplash.com/photos/a-fish-that-is-swimming-in-some-water-TKp2XDjHeGo?utm_content=creditShareLink&utm_medium=referral&utm_source=unsplash

As the world became more technological and industrial, people went on to develop societies that relied a lot on the new systems humans built. During this time, researchers did not think about what impact human decisions would have on the environment. When people expanded their cities, the treatment of Lake Chalco and Lake Xochimilco was a great example of how people sometimes act without thinking about nature. Now that scientists have done more research and know how important these areas are for biodiversity, some changes need to be made so that people can live in harmony with nature.

Since Lake Chalco and Lake Xochimilco are the only places on the planet where axolotls live naturally, the area is important for their survival. Axolotl numbers are rapidly decreasing, so taking care of this region means that this wonderful little lake monster will be able to live on to impress future kids with its cool tricks, like growing back its brain. Scientists are still uncovering many mysteries about how axolotls function, so their habitats can be extremely helpful for learning.

Other than axolotls, plant and animal species found in the area are also important for biodiversity. In the Xochimilco-Chalco basin, 220 plant species grow on land, and 22 grow in water. "Terrestrial plants" are those that grow on land, and "aquatic plants" are those that grow in water. Some of these plant species were introduced by humans because they are not indigenous to the region. Native plants can occasionally become extinct due to the depletion of natural resources and illnesses introduced by foreign plants that native plants are unable to resist. Sometimes, people change ecosystems without realizing it or by mistake, like bringing animals from different continents into new regions by boat.

It is not just plants and animals that are important for the area. If you take a microscope and zoom in a bit closer, you will find tiny little living things called microorganisms. These microorganisms can be divided into two groups, called "zooplankton" and "phytoplankton." Zooplankton are microscopic animals, and phytoplankton are microscopic plants. Even though people cannot see them by using only their eyes, these tiny creatures are super important for the food chains in this unique ecosystem. Many animals feed on microorganisms, and their waste is essential for plant nutrients and improving the quality of soil.

The Xochimilco-Chalco basin is not only special because of its natural biodiversity, but it is also a place to study how ancient cultures in Mexico lived. The Aztec ancestors of modern Mexico constructed farming areas called chinampas. Axolotls used these chinampas as comfortable homes where they could hide from predators and hunt for tasty worms. Chinampas are an example of how humans and nature can work together to benefit everyone. By shifting a few unhealthy habits, people will be able to treat nature better and restore the homes of these beautiful amphibian friends, known as axolotls, along with many other amazing critters.

Living in artificial conditions has changed axolotls. In the wild, these amphibians grow a lot bigger and faster than they do in captivity. This means that their natural environment is much better for them than the artificial habitats humans create for them in labs, zoos, or in their homes when axolotls are kept as pets. In the wild, axolotls often reach 18 inches, but most of them in captivity will max out at 9 inches. This means that their size can be doubled when left to grow and fend for themselves in the wild. The fact that humans cannot create the exact conditions for them to thrive as they do in their natural habitat shows how little people know about the unique region.

Shrinking Axolotl Habitats in the Wild: The Importance of Conservation

Biodiversity means that there is a mixture of a lot of organisms and species in areas or on the planet. "Bio" means life, and "diversity" means a variety of something. So, the best way to understand biodiversity is as a variety of different lifeforms, including plants, animals, insects, and spiders. When habitats of plants or animals shrink, it reduces the biodiversity of the earth. Therefore, having a wide variety of plants and animals is good for many reasons. First, a lack of diversity is linked to the development of new diseases. Second, many communities use natural resources in ways that were taught to them by their forefathers, so getting rid of natural ecosystems also destroys many people's way of life. Lastly, having a lot of natural areas around the world helps decrease global warming and combats climate change.

Conservation means protecting nature, including plants, animals, and all other living organisms. Successful conservation requires people to protect the habitats of endangered species that are only able to thrive in very specific environments, like axolotls. Therefore, governments and businesses need to work together to find ways to reduce the negative impact that humans have on the environment. You can do your part to conserve nature by cleaning up parks and lakes in your area with your parents, teachers, family, and friends. To protect wonderful species like the axolotl, everybody needs to work together.

10. *Conservation means protecting our planet and its species. Source: https://pixabay.com/vectors/recycle-green-earth-environment-29227/*

As humans expand into natural territories, the impact on the world will become clearer. People are already starting to see some of the problems with climate change. Clearing out an area for humans to live and work in means that hundreds of plant and animal species will die. Nobody fully understands what will happen when these unique ecosystems disappear, but you can almost guarantee that it will be terrible for future generations who will have to deal with the illnesses and lack of natural resources that will likely occur. We will also lose a lot more incredible plants and animals, like the axolotl.

Chapter 3: Axolotl Lifestyle and Behavior

The lives of axolotls are exciting and mysterious. Don't be fooled by their cute looks because these guys can get up to a lot of mischief. Understanding how they behave gives people a glimpse into how they developed the unique abilities that they have. This young species is just 10,000 years old and it has a lot of personality. The adaptations have many scientists scratching their heads, trying to understand these beautiful creatures.

11. Axolotls have exciting lives. Source:
https://pixabay.com/photos/axolotl-animal-aquarium-pet-albino-
6870652/

Watching axolotls in their natural habitat is a privilege that only a few people on the planet will ever have. Those lucky few have come back with some interesting behaviors not seen among many other amphibians. Their decreasing numbers in nature caused by pollution, human expansion, and the introduction of invasive species means that it is becoming more difficult to find them in their natural homes.

Their lives in the water are filled with adventure as they hunt for food and avoid predators. The wet wonderland has allowed them to evolve unique traits catered to the limited environment that they inhabit, which is why small changes to their homes have had such a devastating effect on them. These lovable amphibians will no longer be around in nature in just a few years, so it is now more necessary than ever before to change the way that humans treat their habitats, which are perfectly catered to their unique lifestyle.

Explore how axolotls live, eat, and move so that you can better understand why they have such a distinctive appearance and structure. By studying their diets and environments, researchers can get a look behind the curtain of this shy animal that avoids being seen. The more you know about axolotls, the more you want to learn about them. Dive into the muddy waters of their swampy habitat and see how axolotls live their hidden lives.

How Axolotls Live, Eat, and Move

The axolotl has quite a different lifecycle than many other amphibians and salamanders. Most salamanders go through some form of metamorphosis before they reach adulthood. Metamorphosis is when an animal or living thing changes form throughout its life, like a tadpole becoming a frog or a caterpillar turning into a butterfly. Axolotls experience neoteny, which means they will look similar to when they were babies to when they are fully grown, which is odd for many amphibians. The metamorphosis that they experience is only partial because they will keep many of their childhood traits. Some adults that grow big enough will eventually develop lungs, which they will use to get more oxygen into their bigger body when they come up to the surface, but most axolotls do not reach this phase and spend the entirety of their lives underwater, much like a fish, even though they are amphibians. This is why locals sometimes call them "walking fish."

12. *Axolotls remain young for their whole life. Source: MOs810, CC BY-SA 4.0 <https://creativecommons.org/licenses/by-sa/4.0>, via Wikimedia Commons: https://commons.wikimedia.org/wiki/File:Ambystoma_mexicanu m_Gdynia_(aksolotl_meksyka%C5%84ski)_02.jpg*

These cutie pies remain young for their whole life. Most of their breathing is done through the gills on the front of their face (which are there from when they hatch) and through their skin, even though some of the elders in the species have grown lungs. The beginning of the axolotl's interesting life starts when the mother lays her eggs, which she attaches to plants that grow in the water. Although axolotls change and are ready to reproduce as they mature, many of their features stay the same throughout their lives. When you look at a baby axolotl, you can predict what it will look like when it gets older because most of its body parts are already there in some shape or form.

Axolotl eggs take about 10 to 14 days to hatch. The mother abandons the eggs because axolotls do not care for their young. Axolotl females lay a ton of eggs, ranging anywhere from 400 to 1,000 at a time. She impregnates herself with a sperm packet she picks up from the lake floor that the male will leave behind. So many eggs are laid because they do not care for their young, which puts them in more danger to predators. Many of the hatchlings will become food and will not make it to adulthood. They even have to look out for their brothers and sisters because they are highly cannibalistic in their younger years, especially if there are limited resources. Bigger axolotls have no problem eating smaller ones if food is low in their habitat, but this behavior is uncommon once they exit their larvae state.

13. Axolotls hatch and mature quickly. Source: Cedricguppy - Camille Lopard, CC BY-SA 4.0 <https://creativecommons.org/licenses/by-sa/4.0>, via Wikimedia Commons: https://commons.wikimedia.org/wiki/File:Ambystoma_mexicanu m_-_jeunes_tout_juste_%C3%A9clos_01.jpg

Axolotls reach maturity quickly, only taking six months to get to the age where they can mate. Since they spend all their lives in water and very seldom go up to the surface, axolotls are excellent swimmers. Their webbed feet push them forward, and their fin-like tail helps them steer. Their smooth, slimy body is also adapted to the wet environment they live in. Axolotls are only found in freshwater lakes in Mexico, so they are not adapted to survive in oceans.

When axolotls are looking for a partner so that they can reproduce, they do a little courting dance. The male starts the dance by nudging the female with his nose to attract her. If the female is interested, she will nudge the male back. The male releases chemicals during the dance that get the female ready. After their courtship is completed, the female will go in between rocks or some reedy plants to tuck away her eggs in a safe spot. She fertilizes the eggs with the spermatophores (or sperm packets) that the male leaves behind after they have their romantic dance. About 95% of the eggs will hatch, and only 5% won't due either to genetic defects or the environment. Most of these babies will never see adulthood, with only the strongest and smartest surviving.

Axolotl diets are carnivorous, meaning that they survive on meat. When axolotls are not snacking on their own kind, they eat worms, crustaceans, mollusks, and sometimes small fish. Axolotls are not great at defending themselves because they do not have many natural predators, but they are masters at hiding. Axolotls spend their days between reeds and rocks to shield themselves from the sun, and they go out to hunt in the evenings so that their prey cannot easily detect them and so that they can move freely.

The wild is a dangerous place, so axolotls' lifespans are a lot shorter in their natural habitats. In their swampy homes, they live until they are about six years old, but when they are kept as pets in a safer environment, they can live to reach 15 years old. One axolotl in a lab even reached the ripe old age of 25. No matter how much they age, they keep their baby face looking young until they die. Axolotl cells are great at regenerating, which means they can easily grow new cells when hurt or as they age.

14. Axolotls can live up to 15 years in an aquarium. Source: https://www.pexels.com/photo/a-kid-looking-down-at-an axolotl-8838033/

Although axolotls are considered mature after about six months, they will continue growing, only reaching their full size after about two years. They will max out at just over 10 inches, but some of them have grown as big as 15 inches. They tend to grow bigger in the wild than they do in captivity because there is more space, and their environment in the wild is a bit more competitive. In nature, it is all about survival of the fittest, so it makes perfect sense that they would get bigger in that rough environment.

Axolotls are featherweights weighing in at 50 to 250 grams. Their colors range, but they are mostly neutral tones like brown, black, and grey so that they can blend in perfectly with their natural marshy habitat. Sometimes, you'll find albino axolotls, which are bright white, and you'll even find some that are pale pink. These colors are not suited for their homes, so they get picked off by predators. You will only find albino or pink axolotls in pet stores and zoos because people who think they are pretty, breed them to have these exotic colors.

Axolotls are vertebras, meaning they have a backbone much like many other amphibian cousins. Feel your nose and your ears. That soft yet firm material is called cartilage. Axolotls have a soft, squishy body that contains a lot of cartilage. For example, the limbs have no bones but are made of soft cartilage material. This makes their body lighter, and they can easily maneuver into small spaces when they want to escape from predators or hide from the blazing heat of the Mexican sun.

These wonderful creatures do not live in groups, preferring to spend their days swimming and hunting alone. They will only meet up with other axolotls either when they want to mate or if they want to eat them. Their solitary life is part of the reason why they are difficult to locate in the wild, as you will not find many of them swimming together. From birth until death, axolotls will have a lonely life, never truly socializing in a group.

Axolotls have a super sense of smell. They can pick up small chemical changes in the water. The sensitivity of their nose helps them move around and find prey. When they are kept as pets, they need to be put in clean water with no chlorine in it because this will mess up their sensitive skin as well as their finely-tuned nose. That's why it is important to keep nature around you clean because you never know which animals or plants you are hurting by littering.

Unique Traits and Behavior Patterns

Probably one of the most amazing traits that axolotls have is their ability to regrow body parts and organs. They are one of a few animals that can grow back their spinal cord. This ability is why they are so widely studied. Researchers are working toward finding out how they have this amazing skill with hopes that it can one day be used to heal people in hospitals. Axolotls can grow back any part of their body, including their legs, their spine, their organs, and even their brain. In labs, some people have found that they can grow back limbs up to five times perfectly. Every single cell is replaced from bone to soft tissue and muscles. This incredible ability means that axolotls are practically superheroes of the amphibian world. Scientists are still doing all they can to find out exactly how they perform this natural magic trick so that it can be used in medical treatments to benefit humans suffering from all kinds of diseases, like cancer.

Their limited habitat also makes these mysterious creatures special. They are mostly found in two lakes in Mexico —Lake Xochimilco and Lake Chalco, as well as a few other waterways and canals in the country. Axolotls only found in specific areas have led to them becoming endangered as people continuously destroy their natural habitat. Conservation groups are doing all they can to stop this destruction from happening, so maybe in the future, axolotls will live long, happy lives in their swampy homes. However, it is unlikely that we will see axolotls disappear from the planet because they are being bred for research in labs and to be kept as pets. There are some problems with breeding these animals in captivity because their genetic diversity is shrinking, which means they will become weaker, sicker, and even lose the amazing abilities that make people study them.

These salamanders are much bigger than many other species, including some that spend a lot of time on land. They are not the biggest salamander species because this honor goes to the South China Giant Salamander. Unlike many other amphibians, axolotls spend most of their lives in water, and some of them never leave. In some rare cases, mature axolotls will make their way to the surface, but for the most part, you can find them taking a dip in the muddy waters that they love so much.

Another special trait of axolotls is that they are neotenic, which means that many of the traits they have when they are young are still kept until they reach full maturity, like their gills and their limbs. Other salamander species typically look completely different as larvae than they do when they are all grown up. Many salamander species breathe through their skin, but the axolotl has specialized gills on the front of its face that take their cuteness to the next level with their adorable whiskers.

Some local people refer to the axolotl as a "walking fish" because of how much time they spend in the water. Other salamanders leave the water when they exit their larvae and juvenile stages of development, but the axolotl will probably never leave the water. When they are raised in homes, their habitat will be a fish tank because they do not need land to be able to thrive, which makes them different from many other amphibians that will make their way onto dry land at some point in their life cycles.

15. Axolotls are called "walking fish" because of the amount of time they spend in the water. Source: LaDameBucolique, CC0, via Wikimedia Commons: https://commons.wikimedia.org/wiki/File:Axolotl-2193331_1280.webp

Axolotls have an interesting way of hunting. They have tiny teeth that are not even strong enough to cut through human skin. To hunt, axolotls turn into vacuum cleaners, sucking up everything that they want to eat. If it is a creature small enough for an axolotl to eat, then it will likely end up in its belly. They avoid plants and fruits and stick to their delicious, meaty diets. Worms are what they enjoy most as they suck them up on the lake floor.

Most axolotls will reach their full size in two years, but some of them continue growing even after they are mature. This is what makes axolotls exciting because they can be so unpredictable. Researchers have observed axolotls staying in their larvae (or newborn state) for years before developing. Hormones are chemicals inside living creatures that cause certain changes or activities to occur in their body. For example, if you get angry or stressed, hormones will get released that fuel that emotion, making you heat up or causing your heart to beat faster. Hormones are what cause axolotls to grow and change; therefore, in the right environment, axolotls will grow for years. Hormonal and environmental changes determine what the axolotl life cycle will look like.

Life for an axolotl in the wild can get dangerous, which is why they have see-through eyelids. Axolotls close their eyelids to protect their eyes, but they cannot risk losing their vision, so their eyelids are completely transparent. It is difficult to tell whether their eyelids are open or closed when you are just looking at them in an aquarium.

Since axolotls breathe by using their skin and their gills, and in very mature animals, their lungs and toxins in their environment easily affect them. Therefore, pollution in their natural homes has harmed a lot of these friendly critters. The Mexican government is forming laws making it illegal to harm axolotls, but there is still a long way to go. Hopefully, people and axolotls can find a way to live together peacefully outside of zoos and pet shops.

Chapter 4: Life Cycle of Axolotls

Life is like a big, fantastic story with lots of different characters. Every living thing has its unique tale to tell, and one of the most exciting stories in the natural world is that of the axolotl. These aquatic salamanders have a pretty unusual life cycle, and they've found the secret to staying young forever. In this chapter, you'll explore the fascinating life cycle of axolotls, those mysterious water-loving creatures that don't follow the usual rules of growing up and changing.

From Eggs to Adults: The Remarkable Growth Stages

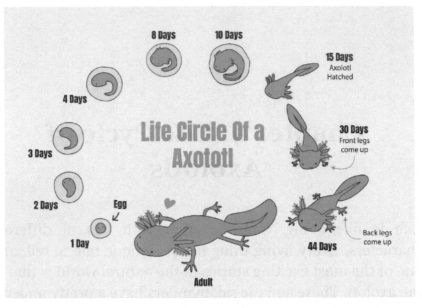

16. *Axolotl life cycle. Source: https://www.shutterstock.com/image-vector/axolotl-life-cycle-1275244015*

Egg Stage

This stage begins when a mature female axolotl lays her eggs in a suitable aquatic environment, such as a pond, lake, or aquarium. The eggs are usually attached to underwater plants or other surfaces. Axolotl eggs are enveloped in a clear, jelly-like substance that serves several crucial purposes.

It provides protection from potential predators, maintains buoyancy, and allows oxygen to diffuse through to the developing embryos. The number of eggs laid by a single female axolotl can vary widely, ranging from dozens to thousands, depending on factors such as the female's age and health.

Hatching

After the eggs are laid, they undergo a period of incubation, which typically lasts around 10 to 14 days, although it can vary depending on environmental conditions like water temperature. During this time, the embryos inside the eggs develop, and the embryos go through a range of developmental changes. When environmental conditions are favorable, and the embryos are ready, the eggs hatch. Small, transparent, and delicate axolotl larvae emerge from the eggs.

Larval Stage

The larval stage is the most defining aspect of the axolotl's life cycle, as they retain their juvenile features and remain aquatic throughout their lives. Axolotl larvae are tiny, typically measuring around 0.5 to 1 inch (1.3 to 2.5 cm) in length when they hatch.

They possess feathery, external gills on the sides of their head, which are used for breathing underwater. These gills are highly efficient at extracting oxygen from the water. Their body shape is adapted for life in the water, with a streamlined form and a large caudal fin on their tail for efficient swimming.

Growth and Development

As axolotl larvae continue to grow, they go through various stages of development over several months. Their size gradually increases, and their limbs and other features become more distinct. While they are small when hatching, they can eventually reach lengths of up to 12 inches (30 cm) or more, depending on factors like food availability and water quality. You'll be reading more about growth and reproduction in the next section.

Reproduction

Axolotls reach sexual maturity at around 18 months to two years of age, although this can vary depending on factors like food availability, water quality, and genetics. When they are ready to reproduce, courtship behaviors come into play. This includes complex dances and movements between male and female axolotls.

During successful courtship, the female axolotl lays her eggs in a safe location, and the male fertilizes them by releasing sperm. This is usually done externally, with the sperm and eggs meeting in the water.

Eternal Youth

One of the most astonishing aspects of axolotls is their apparent immortality and the fact that they never undergo metamorphosis. Unlike most amphibians, which typically undergo metamorphosis in order to transition to a terrestrial adult form, axolotls maintain their aquatic larval form throughout their lives. This means they continue to possess their juvenile features, including external gills and aquatic adaptations, without going through aging or transformation.

The axolotl's life cycle is a fascinating journey marked by their unique ability to stay juvenile and aquatic. This remarkable feature challenges the typical patterns of amphibian development, making axolotls a subject of immense interest in scientific research, particularly in biology and genetics, and a source of inspiration for understanding regeneration and longevity.

Axolotl Reproduction and Growth

Axolotl reproduction is a fascinating process marked by specific behaviors, external fertilization, and egg development.

Courtship

When sexually mature, male and female axolotls engage in complex courtship behaviors. These behaviors may include circling, nuzzling, and even a courtship "dance" in which the male and female swim in circles around each other.

Egg Laying

After successful courtship, the female axolotl will lay her eggs. These eggs are often attached to submerged vegetation or other surfaces in the aquatic environment. A single female axolotl can lay a substantial number of eggs, which can range from several hundred to several thousand in a single reproductive event.

Fertilization

Axolotls rely on external fertilization. The male releases sperm into the water, and the sperm fertilizes the eggs outside the body. This contrasts with some other amphibians that engage in internal fertilization. The mixing of sperm and eggs in the aquatic environment is essential for successful reproduction.

Parental Care

Axolotls do not provide any parental care for their offspring. After fertilization, the development of the embryos is entirely dependent on the external environment. The eggs are not guarded or protected by the parents.

Hatching

The eggs go through an incubation period, which typically lasts around 10 to 14 days, although this period can vary depending on factors like water temperature. When the eggs are ready to hatch, small axolotl larvae emerge.

Growth

Likewise, the growth of axolotls is a crucial part of their life cycle, and they undergo various stages of development. The growth encompasses several processes and changes.

Larval Stage

When axolotl larvae hatch from their eggs, they are small... usually measuring around 0.5 to 1 inch (1.3 to 2.5 cm) in length. At this stage, they maintain the appearance of their juvenile features.

The larval stage of axolotls is a critical and distinctive part of their life cycle. During this stage, axolotls retain their juvenile characteristics and remain fully aquatic.

External Gills

One of the most remarkable features of axolotl larvae is their external gills. These are feathery, bushy structures located on either side of their head. Unlike adult amphibians, such as frogs, axolotls do not develop internal gills or lose their gills as they age. Instead, they retain these external gills throughout their lives. The external gills are highly efficient at extracting oxygen from the water, allowing axolotls to respire underwater.

Caudal Fin

17. Axolotls have caudal fins on their tails. Source: Cedricguppy, CC BY-SA 4.0 <https://creativecommons.org/licenses/by-sa/4.0>, via Wikimedia Commons: https://commons.wikimedia.org/wiki/File:Ambystoma_mexicanum-_triton_du_mexique_wiki14.JPG

Axolotl larvae have a prominent and vertically-flattened caudal fin, which is located at the tail. This fin is large and helps them with swimming and maintaining their buoyancy in the water. It provides the necessary propulsion for their aquatic lifestyle.

Limbs and Digits

During the larval stage, axolotls possess only rudimentary limb buds, which have not yet developed into fully functional limbs with digits (fingers and toes). This is in contrast to other amphibians, which go through metamorphosis, lose their gills, and develop limbs for life on land.

Coloration

Axolotl larvae often display a relatively simple and translucent coloration. They are usually pale in color, with a hint of pink or gray, and their internal organs are often visible through their skin. Their coloration can vary based on factors like genetics, environmental conditions, and diet.

Behavior

Larval axolotls are entirely aquatic and exhibit behaviors suited for this lifestyle. They are proficient swimmers, using their caudal fin to navigate through the water. Their primary activities include hunting small prey, finding shelter in aquatic vegetation, and maintaining their oxygen supply through their external gills.

Feeding

Axolotl larvae are primarily carnivorous and feed on small aquatic invertebrates, larvae, and other small prey. They are opportunistic feeders and adapt their diet based on what is available in their environment.

Development

Over several months, axolotls continue to grow and develop. Their size gradually increases, and they undergo various stages of development. This includes the growth of limbs, the formation of digits (fingers and toes), and the development of other features.

Maturity

Axolotls typically reach maturity at around 18 months to two years of age. However, the exact timing can vary depending on factors like food availability and water quality.

Size

The size of adult axolotls can vary, but they can grow to lengths of up to 12 inches (30 cm) or more, depending on factors such as genetics, food availability, and water quality.

Remarkable Regeneration Abilities

Axolotls are renowned for their extraordinary regenerative capabilities, which set them apart from most other animals. Their regenerative abilities allow them to regrow lost or damaged body parts with remarkable precision. Here's a closer look at their regenerative prowess.

Limb Regeneration

One of the most well-known aspects of axolotl regeneration is their ability to regrow lost limbs. If an axolotl loses a leg or an arm, it can completely regenerate the missing limb, including bones, muscles, blood vessels, and nerves.

The process of limb regeneration begins with the formation of a specialized structure known as a blastema at the site of the injury. The blastema contains cells that can differentiate into the various tissues needed to rebuild the limb.

Spinal Cord Regeneration

Axolotls possess the unique capability of regenerating their spinal cord. If their spinal cord is injured, they can regrow the damaged portion and restore lost functions.

This regenerative process involves the reestablishment of neural connections and the regeneration of spinal cord tissue, which is a significant focus of scientific research due to its potential implications for treating spinal cord injuries in humans.

Heart Regeneration

Axolotls can also regrow parts of their heart. In experiments, if a portion of their heart is surgically removed, they can regenerate the missing cardiac tissue. This ability is of great interest to researchers studying heart regeneration, and it holds potential insights for improving cardiac regenerative therapies for humans.

Brain Regeneration

Axolotls have demonstrated the capacity to regenerate parts of their brain. Studies have shown that they can recover lost brain tissue and regain lost functions, such as memory and sensory perception. This brain regeneration ability is of particular significance in neuroscience and regenerative medicine.

Tail Regeneration

Axolotls can also regenerate their tail if they are injured or severed. The regrown tail is typically identical in structure and function to the original one. Tail regeneration is another area of interest for researchers, as it provides insights into regenerative processes that can be applied to other species.

Skin and Tissue Regeneration

Beyond major body parts, axolotls can also regenerate their skin, cartilage, and various tissues with high efficiency. This contributes to their overall regenerative abilities and resilience.

Genetic Factors

Genetic factors play a significant role in axolotl regeneration. Their unique genetic makeup and the presence of specific genes are thought to underpin their remarkable regenerative abilities. Researchers are studying these genetic factors to better understand the molecular mechanisms involved in regeneration and to potentially apply this knowledge to human regenerative medicine.

Conservation Status and Threats

IUCN Classification

The International Union for Conservation of Nature (IUCN) classifies axolotls as "Critically Endangered." This is the highest level of endangerment, and it indicates a very high risk of extinction in the wild.

Habitat Range

Axolotls are native to the ancient lake systems of Xochimilco and Chalco in Mexico. These unique habitats, characterized by a system of canals and wetlands, are crucial for axolotl survival.

Population Decline

Over the past century, the wild population of axolotls has experienced a dramatic decline. In the early 20th century, axolotls were abundant in their native habitat; however, multiple factors have contributed to their decline.

Threats to Axolotls

Habitat Destruction

Habitat destruction is one of the most significant threats to axolotls. The draining of the Xochimilco and Chalco lake systems for agriculture, urban expansion, and infrastructure development has led to a significant reduction in their natural habitat. The loss of these unique wetland ecosystems has been detrimental to axolotl populations.

Pollution

18. *Pollution degrades the water quality in axolotl habitats. Source: https://pixabay.com/illustrations/pollution-garbage-degradation-1603644/*

Pollution from various sources, including agricultural runoff, industrial discharges, and untreated sewage, has severely degraded the water quality in axolotl habitats. Elevated pollution levels can harm both axolotls and their prey, impacting their health and reproduction.

Invasive Species

The introduction of non-native fish species, such as tilapia and carp, into axolotl habitats has had adverse effects. These invasive fish species compete with axolotls for food resources and may even prey on axolotl larvae, further endangering their survival.

Climate Change

Climate change can indirectly affect axolotls by altering the environmental conditions in their habitats. Changes in water temperature, oxygen levels, and weather patterns can have significant impacts on axolotls' health, behavior, and reproduction.

Illegal Collection

Axolotls have been subject to illegal collection for the pet trade and for use in scientific research. Despite regulations designed to protect wild axolotls, illegal collection remains a concern, leading to further population decline.

Conservation Efforts

Captive Breeding Programs

Many institutions and conservation organizations have established captive breeding programs to ensure the survival of axolotls in controlled environments. These programs focus on maintaining genetically diverse populations.

Habitat Restoration

Conservationists and government agencies are working to restore and protect the remaining axolotl habitats in the Xochimilco and Chalco lake systems. This includes efforts to reduce pollution, restore wetland ecosystems, and create conditions suitable for axolotls to thrive.

Research and Education

Research on axolotls, their biology, and their genetics is vital for understanding their unique traits and for developing conservation strategies. Education and awareness campaigns play a role in garnering public support for axolotl conservation.

Legislation and Protection

Mexico has implemented laws and regulations to safeguard axolotls and their habitats. These include the prohibition of capturing wild axolotls for the pet trade.

Collaboration

International and local collaboration among researchers, conservationists, and government agencies is essential for developing and implementing effective conservation measures. Coordinated efforts are necessary to address the complex challenges faced by axolotls.

The axolotl's life cycle is a captivating journey marked by its unique ability to maintain a juvenile, aquatic form throughout its life. This feature challenges the typical patterns of amphibian development and aging, making axolotls subjects of immense interest in scientific research and a source of inspiration for understanding regeneration and longevity.

Moreover, in the larval stage, axolotls exhibit remarkable external gills, a caudal fin, and the retention of juvenile features. These traits, coupled with their unique neoteny and regenerative abilities, contribute to their fascination in the realm of biology and regenerative medicine.

Axolotls' unparalleled regenerative abilities are truly astounding, enabling them to regrow lost or damaged body parts such as limbs, the spinal cord, the heart, the brain, and various tissues. Their regenerative prowess has made them invaluable subjects for scientific research, offering potential implications for regenerative therapies in humans.

Nonetheless, the conservation status of axolotls is dire, with the species being classified as critically endangered. This status stems from habitat destruction, pollution, invasive species, climate change, and illegal collection. To ensure the survival of these unique creatures and their significance in scientific and ecological contexts, ongoing conservation efforts, including captive breeding, habitat restoration, research, and legal protection, are essential. These actions are imperative to preserving the axolotl's unique life cycle and its contribution to our understanding of regeneration and longevity.

Chapter 5: Axolotls in the Ecosystem

Despite their unusual appearance, axolotls play a vital role in aquatic habitats. In this chapter, you'll unravel the mysteries of these fascinating creatures, exploring their role and remarkable contributions to aquatic environments.

The Role of Axolotls in Aquatic Environments

Axolotls' distinctive external gills, fringed crests, and feathery appearance are well-adapted to their aquatic lifestyles. Their role in aquatic environments is multifaceted and critical to maintaining the delicate balance of these ecosystems. Here's a closer look at the critical aspects of their role.

19. *Axolotls play an interesting role in their ecosystem. Source: Emőke Dénes, CC BY-SA 4.0 <https://creativecommons.org/licenses/by-sa/4.0>, via Wikimedia Commons: https://commons.wikimedia.org/wiki/File:Ke_-_Ambystoma mexicanum_-_6.jpg*

Predator-Prey Dynamics

Feeding Behavior: Axolotls are skilled predators, using their keen senses to hunt for food. They mainly feed on small aquatic invertebrates like insects, crustaceans, and even smaller vertebrates.

Population Control: Axolotls help control the population of these prey species. By keeping the numbers of smaller creatures in check, they prevent overpopulation, which could otherwise disrupt the balance of the aquatic ecosystem.

Supporting Biodiversity: Through predatory behavior, axolotls indirectly support the diversity of life in their habitat. They contribute to a healthier and more varied ecosystem by preventing a single species from dominating.

Nutrient Cycling

Waste Products: As axolotls feed and digest their food, they produce waste in the form of feces. This waste contains essential nutrients that are returned to the water.

Nutrient Contribution: The nutrients in axolotl waste are released into the water and become available for other organisms. Aquatic plants and phytoplankton can absorb these nutrients and use them to grow.

This process supports primary productivity in the ecosystem, as it provides a source of nutrients for the foundation of the food web, which includes plant life.

Indicator Species

Sensitivity to Environmental Changes: Axolotls are sensitive to changes in water quality and habitat conditions. They are often regarded as indicator species, which means their presence or absence indicates the overall health of an aquatic environment.

Monitoring Ecosystem Health: Scientists and conservationists use axolotls as indicators to monitor the well-being of their habitat. If axolotl populations are stable, it suggests a healthy ecosystem. If they start disappearing, it can signal environmental problems, such as pollution or habitat destruction.

Sustaining Ecosystem Balance

Preventing Overgrazing: Axolotls consume smaller creatures to prevent certain species from overgrazing on aquatic vegetation. This helps maintain a balanced food web, preventing vegetation from being completely consumed.

Controlling Prey Populations: By regulating the populations of invertebrates and other smaller vertebrates, axolotls indirectly influence the abundance of their prey. This, in turn, affects the predators that rely on these smaller creatures for sustenance.

By keeping prey populations in check, axolotls contribute to the overall health of the aquatic ecosystem. This balance helps ensure that no species dominates or disrupts the natural order of the environment.

With their unique position as both predator and prey in the aquatic food web, axolotls play an integral role in maintaining the health and diversity of their underwater homes. Their role as nutrient contributors, their sensitivity to environmental changes, and their population control mechanisms collectively contribute to the delicate balance of the aquatic ecosystems they inhabit.

How They Contribute to Habitats

Habitat Engineering

Axolotls are known for their burrowing behavior. They create burrows in the substrate of their aquatic habitats, including mud or soft sediments.

Oxygenation of Sediment

These burrows serve a dual purpose. As axolotls dig and move about, they help oxygenate the sediment. This is a crucial process as it prevents the buildup of toxic gases, making the aquatic environment a better place for other species to thrive.

Shelter for Other Species

The burrows benefit axolotls and shelter other tiny aquatic organisms, like young fish and aquatic invertebrates. This shelter protects them from predators.

Preventing Overgrazing

By consuming a variety of prey species, axolotls help prevent overgrazing by certain aquatic invertebrates. Without axolotls, these smaller creatures could consume excessive amounts of aquatic vegetation.

Balanced Food Web

Axolotls, as predators, play a crucial role in regulating the population of their prey. This contributes to the balanced structure of the aquatic food web, where no single species dominates or disrupts the natural order.

Genetic Diversity

Regenerative Abilities

Axolotls have amazing regeneration powers; they can recover missing limbs, spinal cords, and even portions of their hearts and brains. Researchers have been captivated by their regeneration potential and have been motivated to replicate their qualities, primarily through genetics and regenerative medicine. Knowing how they accomplish this regeneration has the potential to alter human standards of care.

Interactions with Other Species

Symbiotic Relationships

Algae and Axolotls: Axolotls can form a symbiotic relationship with algae. Algae can grow on the skin of axolotls

---

without harming them. In return, the algae benefit from the nutrients and protection provided by the axolotl's skin.

20. Algae can grow on axolotls without harming them. Source: LoKiLeCh, CC BY-SA 3.0 <http://creativecommons.org/licenses/by-sa/3.0/>, via Wikimedia Commons: https://commons.wikimedia.org/wiki/File:Axolotl_Portrait.jpg

Complementary Survival: This relationship is mutually beneficial. The algae gain a place to thrive and access sunlight, while axolotls receive camouflage and potential access to some additional nutrients.

Competition with Fish Species

Resource Competition: In habitats where axolotls coexist with fish species, there can be competition for resources, such as food and shelter. Fish may prey on similar invertebrates, potentially impacting the food supply available to axolotls.

Habitat Competition: The burrows created by axolotls can also be used by some fish species for shelter. This can lead to competition for these burrows, affecting both the axolotls and the fish.

Predation on Axolotls

Birds of Prey: Birds like herons and egrets are known to prey on axolotls. These birds wade in the water and can spot axolotls due to their distinctive appearance.

Fish Predators: Some fish species, especially larger ones, may feed on axolotls if they encounter them in their habitat. The presence of fish predators can impact the distribution and behavior of axolotls.

Prey for Larger Aquatic Predators

Chain of Predation: Axolotls themselves are prey for larger aquatic predators. They are part of a chain of predation in their ecosystem.

Contributing to Food Webs: By serving as a food source for larger predators, axolotls contribute to the energy flow and nutrient cycling within the aquatic food web.

Aquatic Invertebrates and Detritivores

Interaction with Detritivores: Axolotls interact with aquatic invertebrates and detritivores (organisms that feed on dead organic matter). Detritivores help break down organic material in the water, which, in turn, can influence the nutrient content of the environment.

Axolotls engage in various interactions with other species in their aquatic ecosystems. These interactions can be both cooperative, such as their symbiotic relationship with algae, as well as competitive, as seen in resource competition with fish species. Additionally, axolotls serve as both predators and prey, contributing to the complex web of life in their habitat. Understanding these interactions is essential for comprehending their ecological role and the dynamics of the ecosystems they inhabit.

Human Influence on Axolotl Habitats

Urbanization

21. Urbanization can cause habitat destruction. Source : https://pixabay.com/vectors/urban-city-sightseeing-tourist-161706/

Habitat Destruction: The expansion of urban areas and infrastructure development often results in the destruction and fragmentation of natural habitats where axolotls reside. Urbanization can lead to the draining and filling of wetlands, which are critical axolotl habitats.

Pollution: Urban areas can introduce pollution in the form of sewage, chemicals, and trash into the aquatic environments where axolotls live. Pollution can negatively impact water quality and the health of axolotls.

Agriculture

Agricultural Runoff: The use of fertilizers and pesticides in agriculture can lead to nutrient runoff into water bodies. Excess nutrients can trigger algal blooms, which deplete oxygen levels in the water and negatively affect axolotls.

Habitat Conversion: Agricultural expansion can result in the conversion of natural habitats into farmland, reducing available habitats for axolotls.

Aquatic Invasive Species

Introduction of Predators: The release of non-native fish species into axolotl habitats can introduce new predators that pose a threat to axolotls. Predatory fish can significantly impact axolotl populations.

Competing Species: Invasive aquatic plants and invertebrates can out-compete native aquatic vegetation, reducing the availability of suitable habitats for axolotls.

Water Extraction and Pollution

Water Extraction: The extraction of water for human consumption, agriculture, and industrial use can alter the water levels in axolotl habitats. Changes in water levels can disrupt the breeding and feeding patterns of axolotls.

Chemical Pollution: Industrial pollutants and chemical contaminants that enter water bodies can directly harm axolotls by affecting their health and reproductive capabilities.

Non-Sustainable Harvesting

Pet Trade: Axolotls are popular in the pet trade, both domestically and internationally. Overharvesting for the pet trade, especially without sustainable practices, can deplete wild populations.

Traditional Medicine: In some regions, axolotls are used in traditional medicine. Unregulated harvesting for this purpose can further stress wild populations.

Climate Change

22. Climate change affects the thermal conditions in axolotl habitats. Source: https://pixabay.com/illustrations/iceberg-ice-arctic-snow-1321692/

Climate change can lead to alterations in temperature and precipitation patterns, affecting the thermal and hydrological conditions in axolotl habitats. Increased frequency and severity of extreme weather events, such as droughts and storms can impact the availability of water and the stability of axolotl habitats.

Human activities, including urbanization, agriculture, the introduction of invasive species, water extraction, non-sustainable harvesting, and climate change have significant effects on axolotl habitats. Understanding and mitigating these influences is crucial for the conservation and preservation of axolotl populations and their natural environments.

Habitat Loss

One of the most significant challenges facing axolotls is the loss of their natural habitat due to urbanization and agriculture. Wetland destruction and habitat degradation have a direct impact on their populations. Efforts are being made to protect and restore axolotl habitats. This includes the creation of protected areas and wetland conservation projects in order to maintain critical breeding and foraging areas.

Pollution

Pollution from human activities, such as sewage, chemicals, and trash, can severely harm axolotls and the aquatic ecosystems they inhabit. Poor water quality can impact their health and reproductive success. Conservationists and local authorities are working to reduce pollution in axolotl habitats. This involves implementing water treatment measures, regulating chemical use, and raising awareness about pollution prevention.

Invasive Species

Non-native species, especially predatory fish and invasive plants, can disrupt axolotl habitats and out-compete native species. Efforts to control and remove invasive species are ongoing. This may involve the removal of predatory fish, the restoration of native vegetation, and the implementation of monitoring programs to prevent further introductions.

Overharvesting

The collection of axolotls for the pet trade and for traditional medicine can lead to overharvesting and a decline in wild populations. Conservation organizations are advocating for sustainable harvesting practices and the regulation of the pet trade. Captive breeding programs have been established to reduce pressure on wild populations and support their recovery.

Climate Change

Climate change can alter temperature and precipitation patterns, impacting the availability of suitable habitats for axolotls. Extreme weather events can be particularly detrimental. Efforts to address climate change impacts on axolotls include climate-resilient habitat restoration and conservation planning. Adaptation strategies aim to provide axolotls with habitat options that can withstand changing conditions.

Genetic Diversity

Due to the small and fragmented wild populations, axolotls face a genetic diversity challenge. Inbreeding and genetic bottlenecks can lead to reduced fitness and adaptability. Breeding programs are established to maintain genetic diversity among captive axolotls. These programs are critical for conserving the genetic potential of the species.

Research and Education

23. Not many are educated about axolotls and their conservation needs. Source: https://pixabay.com/vectors/boy-book-reding-child-school-311392/

A lack of public awareness and understanding about axolotls and their conservation needs can hinder efforts to protect them. Educational programs and outreach initiatives are in place to raise awareness about axolotls and their importance in ecosystems. Public engagement is a vital component of conservation efforts.

Legal Protection

In some regions, axolotls lack legal protection, making it challenging to enforce conservation measures and prevent their exploitation. Advocacy for legal protection is ongoing. Scientists and conservation organizations are working to secure legal status for axolotls, which would grant them greater protection from harmful activities.

Addressing the conservation challenges facing axolotls involves a combination of habitat protection, pollution control, invasive species management, sustainable harvesting practices, climate change adaptation, genetic diversity conservation, public awareness, and legal safeguards. Efforts to safeguard axolotls are critical for the continued survival of this unique amphibian and the health of its aquatic ecosystems.

Chapter 6: Fun Axolotl Facts and Activities

Do you think you have learned everything about axolotls? You aren't even close. These small creatures are just as interesting as they look, and there are still many things about them to cover. You are about to discover some fun, strange, and crazy facts about axolotls that will make you even more interested in them. There are also some activities in the end to make arts and crafts of your favorite creature.

24. There are many fun facts related to axolotls. Source: https://unsplash.com/photos/a-fish-that-is-swimming-in-some-water-TKp2XDjHeGo?utm_content=creditShareLink&utm_medium=referral&utm_source=unsplash

Fascinating Facts about Axolotls

Are you ready to know more about axolotls? Be careful... after this part, you will know so much about axolotls that you will not be able to stop talking about them.

What's in a Name?

The axolotl is a unique game, right? Do you know there is an interesting story behind it? There was once an ancient culture called the Aztecs who believed that axolotls were a representation of the god of death, Xolotl. Because of axolotls' regeneration abilities and interesting looks, the Aztecs believed they were divine. In one story, Xolotl was afraid he would die, so he transformed into an axolotl. This is how they got their awesome name. The name "Axolotl" means "water dog" since Xolotl had a dog's head.

The Aztecs used to eat axolotls because they believed axolotls could cure them of many diseases.

Dance Moves

Axolotls are ready to mate and have babies when they turn six months old. So, how do male and female axolotls express their feelings to each other? Well, they don't send text messages. They move together in circles that look like a waltz dance. Romantic... right?

Forever Young

Axolotls look like babies all their lives. They have the same face, body, and gills. Just like babies, they never have teeth. Nothing about them changes from the moment they are born till they die.

However, they can grow up with the help of science. If a scientist gives an axolotl a shot of iodine, it can suddenly grow up and become mature. However, it is always best to leave these small creatures alone to have a normal life cycle and grow naturally.

No Chewing

Since axolotls don't have teeth, they don't chew their food. They feed by sucking the food into their mouth. They stay babies all their lives.

Lone Wolves

Although most animals and fish prefer to be in packs, axolotls are lone wolves. They don't run in groups, and males and females don't spend time together after mating. They love to be alone. They are considered friendly creatures; however, they just aren't big fans of socializing.

If you plan to have them as pets, you should keep axolotls in an aquarium alone without other fish. They will eat the smaller fish, and the bigger fish can attack them.

Smiley Face

25. Axolotls look like they're smiling in most pictures. Source: https://unsplash.com/photos/a-close-up-of-an-animal-on-a-bed-of-rocks-DTwn4h5HJ-U?utm_content=creditShareLink&utm_medium=referral&utm_source=unsplash

Have you wondered why axolotls smile in all their pictures? Well, they aren't really smiling. Their lips stay open for a few seconds after they finish their meal, giving the impression that they are grinning. Some types of axolotls also have turned-up lips, which give them that cheerful look.

Axolotls Emoji

In 2017, Mexico held an emoji contest and asked people to create symbols that represent their city. The winner created a package that had symbols of axolotls. This shows the popularity and importance of axolotls in Mexico and how much the people love them.

In 2022, they even added a picture of an axolotl on their 50-peso banknote.

Big Appetite

Axolotls eat everything, even meat and other fish. They aren't really picky eaters.

Lifespan

In the wild, axolotls can live up to six years. However, as pets, they can live much longer — for about 15 years since there are usually fewer threats.

Pretty Colors

It isn't just their smiling faces that make axolotls look pretty... they also have very beautiful colors. Their genes are responsible for these intriguing colors. In the wild, axolotls are often brown or black with gold or olive patches. Do you want to know something really cool? Axolotls camouflage by changing colors so they can disappear whenever they want to hide.

Growing Body Parts

Axolotls have a unique ability to regenerate or regrow their tail, skin, parts of their heart, brain, and other parts of their body. They don't do this just once or twice, but five times in their lives. Although other amphibians can regenerate their limbs or tail, none of them can regenerate every part of their body, like axolotls. So, if they lose an arm or a leg, they can grow another one back in a couple of weeks. How awesome is that?

Unique DNA

Axolotls have a large and pretty unique DNA. Scientists are very interested and curious about it. They hope to find out how the axolotls regenerate so they can help those who lost an arm or a leg. In fact, many scientists believe that axolotls' DNA can help find a cure for cancer.

So Many Eggs

Do you know that female axolotls lay from 100 to 1,000 eggs? However, they don't stay around after the process. Once a female axolotl lays her eggs, she leaves. When they hatch, the babies have no adults around to look after them, so they must take care of themselves. This really shows how much they love being alone.

Eating Axolotls

This can be hard to believe, but some people eat these adorable creatures. Since axolotls have become an endangered species (they are at risk of becoming extinct), many people have stopped eating them. However, there are still restaurants in Japan that serve them.

Males vs. Females

You can easily tell the difference between male and female axolotls. Male axolotls don't have eyelids, and they have a wide and large head and a long tail. Female axolotls have a round body and a smaller tail than males.

Very Small

26. Axolotls are almost the same size as a guinea pig. Source: https://www.pexels.com/photo/landscape-nature-animal-cute-63853/

Axolotls are very small creatures. They are usually between 8 and 11 inches long — the same size as an envelope or a guinea pig.

Sweet Creatures

Axolotls are just as sweet as they look. They aren't harmful to humans or contain toxic substances.

Eyes Open

Since axolotls don't have eyelids, they sleep with their eyes open. If you have a pet axolotl, it will be impossible to know if they are awake or asleep. However, axolotls usually sleep all day and are active and awake at night. If their gills aren't moving or if they are hiding, they are probably asleep.

Gills

Axolotls have gills like all other fish, but they are on the sides of their head, and they have a feathery look. They also have lungs and often rise to the surface of the water to get some fresh air.

Mexico

27. Wild axolotls can only be found in Mexico. Source: https://pixabay.com/illustrations/mexico-flag-grunge-north-america-1242251/

Interestingly, you will only find wild axolotls in Mexico. They don't exist anywhere else in the world.

Cold Water

Axolotls love cold water, and they live better in it. If you have a pet axolotl, lower their water temperature or cool it down during the summer. They can get stressed and even sick in warm water.

Chemical Communication

Although axolotls prefer to be alone and don't need the company of others, they sometimes communicate with one another. They do this by sending chemical signals that another axolotl picks up and responds to it. They usually send these signals when one of them finds prey and wants to invite the others to join it.

Cool Nickname

Mexicans call axolotls "Walking Fish" because they look like fish and have toes on both feet.

Extinction

Sadly, axolotls are at risk of going extinct. There are only about 1,000 left. Luckily, there are many groups working hard to protect the remaining axolotls from extinction.

Predators

One of the reasons why axolotls are at risk of extinction is because of predators. There are many creatures in the sea that feed on them, like perch and tilapia fish. Certain types of birds also swoop into the water and eat axolotls.

They Bite

Although axolotls don't have teeth, they can bite. It is nothing serious or painful... they just latch onto you with their mouth without causing any damage. Their bites are usually a warning that you have entered their private space and should take a step back.

They Can't See

Axolotls aren't blind; they just can't see very well, so they usually depend on their sense of smell when they are looking for food.

Nibbling on Their Siblings

Other threats that axolotls face are from other axolotls. Yes, you read that correctly. Axolotls sometimes feed on one another. A young axolotl would happily eat their brother's or sister's hand or leg. Luckily, since they regenerate and their body parts regrow, there isn't usually any permanent damage.

Great Pets

No surprise here, but this cute fish with a baby face and beautiful colors makes a great pet. If you are planning to bring an axolotl home, you should take good care of it because it is a fragile creature. Keep it in a big aquarium and feed it snails and worms.

Fun Activities

Now that you have learned everything about axolotls, are you ready for some fun activities?

Draw

Tools:

- A piece of paper or a sketchbook.
- Crayons

Instructions:

1. Look at any of the axolotl pictures in a book.
2. Draw an axolotl like the picture and color it.

Story

Tools:

- A piece of paper.
- A Pencil

- Crayons

Instructions:

1. Use the information you learned in the book and write a story about an axolotl and its adventure in the water.

2. You can add some axolotl drawings as well to your story.

Axolotls Jumble

Tools:

- Glue or tape.
- Pencils and erasers.
- Sheets of paper.

Instructions:

Play this game with your friends or brothers and sisters.

1. Each one of you will draw a different body part of the axolotl.

2. Agree with each other on the part you want to draw, like one can draw the head, another will draw the gills, and someone else will draw the body.

3. After you all finish, glue the body parts together.

An Axolotl Sticky Wall

Tools:

- Contact paper
- Painter's tape
- Whiteboard
- Colorful straws

- Scissors

Instructions:

1. Draw a big axolotl on the whiteboard.

2. Cover the whiteboard with the contact paper.

3. Cut the straws into small pieces and put them on the board as gills.

Axolotl Valentine's Card

Tools:

- Scissors

- Glue stick

- Card (any color).

- Pen

- A large, oval piece of paper (draw an oval shape and cut it).

- Axolotl paws (just cut two small pieces of paper).

- 6 gills (cut 6 pieces of paper shaped like a small finger).

- The axolotl body (draw it on a piece of paper, then cut it).

- 5 small heart shapes (draw 5 hearts on red paper and cut it).

N.B. If you can't cut these shapes, you can print an axolotl template and print the hearts online.

Instructions:

1. Fold the hearts in half. You can write something on one of the hearts if you want.

2. Put glue on half of the first heart.

3. Put the second heart on top of the glued part of the first heart.

4. Put glue on the second heart, then put the third heart on it.

5. Do the same with the fourth and fifth hearts (the one you wrote on) in order to have a set of hearts that open up.

6. Glue the gills to the back of the head (three on each side).

7. Fold the body part in half.

8. Glue the head on top of the body part.

9. Glue one paw to the first heart and the other paw to the fifth heart and stick them together.

10. Put glue on the back of the paws and hearts, and put them on top of the body.

11. Draw an axolotl on the oval head (just draw two eyes and a mouth).

Toilet Roll Axolotl

Tools:

- One toilet paper roll.
- Glue
- Brush and paint (any color you want).
- Scrap paper
- Markers

Instructions:

1. Paint the toilet paper roll and leave it to dry.

2. Squeeze one side of the roll to make a little flap that inverts, then flatten it.

3. Then, repeat on the other side.

4. Cut the scrap paper to make six gills... make them oval.

5. Glue three on each side of the roll of paper.

6. Draw an axolotl face with the marker.

Paper Plate Axolotl

Tools:

- A paper plate
- Paint (choose the color you want).
- Googly eyes
- Glue
- Marker
- Scissors

Instructions:

1. Paint the paper plate.

2. Let the paint dry.

3. Glue the googly eyes on the plate.

4. Draw the mouth with the marker.

Egg Carton Axolotl

Tools:

- Egg carton
- Paintbrush and paint.
- Googly eyes

- Red pipe cleaners.
- Scissors

Instructions:

1. Cut out two sections of the egg carton.

2. Paint the carton and leave it to dry.

3. Glue on the googly eyes, then draw the face with a black marker.

4. Cut six pipelines to make the gills.

5. Glue three on each side.

Stick Axolotl

Tools:

- Paint
- 5 craft sticks.
- Glue
- Black Sharpie
- Red pipe cleaners.
- Pink paper
- Scissors

Instructions:

1. Make the axolotl body by lining up four sticks.

2. Cut the fifth stick in half, and glue a half on top of the four sticks and the other half at the bottom to glue the four sticks together.

3. Turn it over, then paint it.

4. Draw an axolotl with the black sharpie on the pink paper.

5. Cut the red pipe cleaners into small pieces to make the gills.

6. When the paint dries, glue the axolotl face on the top of the sticks.

7. Glue the stick on the other side.

If you are struggling with any of these activities, ask your parents or older siblings to help you. In fact, it will be fun to do these activities together as a family. They may even love the axolotl like you.

You can hang any of these crafts in your room or give the card to a friend or to your parents.

Axolotls are cute and interesting creatures. They are colorful and look like they are always smiling. Who doesn't love them? If you love these facts and activities, share them with your friends and turn them into axolotl fans just like you.

Conclusion

Who doesn't love axolotls? They are cute little fish with adorable faces and an interesting look, and they are really awesome. No wonder you wanted to learn everything about them. This book took you on a fascinating journey into the world of axolotls, where you discovered many cool things about them.

You started this journey by learning about axolotls and what makes them so special. You probably had a lot of questions about them, like where do they live? What do their lives look like? You have answers to all your questions and more.

You then got into their fascinating world and learned about their behavior and lifestyle. You found out how they live and move and what they eat. It was like you were living with them. You also discovered how they behave, what their personality is like, and all the traits that make them unique.

You then learned about their life cycle from the moment they are tiny babies in their mother's eggs until they are all grown up. You saw every stage of their life and their amazing growth journey. You also learned how these sweet creatures reproduce.

You then learned about their ecosystem, their role in their environment, and how they help other water creatures. You discovered many interesting things about their life and saw their importance in the environment.

You then got to the funnest part of the book. You learned some fun and interesting facts about axolotls that made you love them even more. You also had fun playing around with the exciting activities at the end.

Axolotls are interesting creatures for many reasons. With their dances and fascinating history, you will never get enough of them. Don't you wish there were more creatures like them?

Did you enjoy reading the book? Don't forget to leave a review.

References

(N.d.). A-z-animals.com. https://a-z-animals.com/blog/axolotl-lifespan-how-long-do-they-live/

(N.d.). A-z-animals.com. https://a-z-animals.com/blog/10-incredible-axolotl-facts/

(N.d.-a). A-z-animals.com. https://a-z-animals.com/blog/axolotl-as-a-pet-the-ultimate-guide-to-caring-for-your-axolotl/

(N.d.-b). Worldwildlife.org. https://www.worldwildlife.org/magazine/issues/summer-2021/articles/meet-the-peter-pan-of-salamanders-the-axolotl

17 astonishing axolotl (Mexican walking fish) facts. (2018, September 16). Fact Animal. https://factanimal.com/axolotl/

Ambystoma mexicanum (Salamandra ajolote). (n.d.). Animal Diversity Web. https://animaldiversity.org/accounts/Ambystoma_mexicanum/

Ambystoma mexicanum, Mexican Axolotls. (n.d.). Uwlax.edu. http://bioweb.uwlax.edu/bio203/s2008/osuldsen_brit/reproduction.html

Art, R. T. (2023a, January 10). Axolotl toilet roll craft for preschoolers. Red Ted Art - Kids Crafts. https://www.redtedart.com/axolotl-toilet-roll-craft/

Art, R. T. (2023b, January 10). Axolotl toilet roll craft for preschoolers. Red Ted Art - Kids Crafts. https://www.redtedart.com/axolotl-toilet-roll-craft/

Art, R. T. (2023c, January 24). 3d Axolotl Valentines Card for kids. Red Ted Art - Kids Crafts. https://www.redtedart.com/diy-axolotl-valentines-card/

Art, R. T. (2023d, January 24). 3d Axolotl Valentines Card for kids. Red Ted Art - Kids Crafts. https://www.redtedart.com/diy-axolotl-valentines-card/

Axolotl facts for kids. (2020, December 31). Animal Fact Guide. https://animalfactguide.com/animal-facts/axolotl/

Axolotl facts for kids: Endangered amphibian info, pictures & video. (2016, December 14). Active Wild. https://www.activewild.com/axolotl-facts-for-kids/

Axolotl. (2018a, March 13). Animalfunfacts.net. https://www.animalfunfacts.net/salamanders/2-axolotl.html

Axolotl. (2018b, November 16). Detroit Zoo; Detroit Zoological Society. https://detroitzoo.org/animals/zoo-animals/mexican-axolotl/

axolotl. (n.d.). In Encyclopedia Britannica.

Axolotl. (n.d.). Sandiegozoo.org. https://animals.sandiegozoo.org/animals/axolotl

Axolotl. (n.d.). Sandiegozoo.org. https://animals.sandiegozoo.org/animals/axolotl

Axolotl. (n.d.). Seaworld.org. https://seaworld.org/animals/facts/amphibians/axolotl/

Axolotl. (n.d.). Torontozoo.com. https://www.torontozoo.com/animals/Axolotl

Axolotl: Threats to its conservation – StMU research scholars. (n.d.). Stmuscholars.org. https://stmuscholars.org/axolotl-threats-to-conservation/

Daisy. (2015, February 26). March in place. SPOTEBI. https://www.spotebi.com/exercise-guide/march-in-place/

Domínguez-Alfaro, N. N. (2023). Xochimilco Lake, Mexico. The importance of its preservation: challenges and opportunities. Researchgate.net. https://www.researchgate.net/publication/368574623_Xochimilc o_Lake_Mexico_The_importance_of_its_preservation_challenge s_and_opportunities

Dunning, H. (n.d.). Axolotls: Meet the amphibians that never grow up. Nhm.ac.uk. https://www.nhm.ac.uk/discover/axolotls-amphibians-that-never-grow-up.html

Dunning, H. (n.d.). Axolotls: Meet the amphibians that never grow up. Nhm.ac.uk. https://www.nhm.ac.uk/discover/axolotls-amphibians-that-never-grow-up.html

ED_PortSmoutH. (2020, October 30). What is an axolotl and why are they endangered? Blue Reef Aquarium. https://www.bluereefaquarium.co.uk/portsmouth/blog/education /what-is-an-axolotl-and-why-are-they-endangered/

Gonzalez, W. (2023, January 14). The role of axolotls in their natural ecosystem. AxolotlKingdom. https://axolotlkingdom.com/the-role-of-axolotls-in-their-natural-ecosystem/

Hawk, M. (2021, May 14). 23 Amazing Axolotl Facts (that You may not know). Animal Nerdz. https://animalnerdz.com/axolotl-facts/

Kirkpatrick, N. (2018, February 20). 8 fascinating facts about the axolotl. Treehugger. https://www.treehugger.com/things-you-dont-know-about-axolotl-4863490

Knibb, F. (2023, August 22). 23 axolotl facts for kids. Deep Sea World. https://www.deepseaworld.com/animal-behaviour/23-axolotl-facts-for-kids/

Lenard. (2021, January 31). Axolotl facts. Facts.net. https://facts.net/axolotl-facts/

Lexi, W. by. (2023, March 6). The fascinating life cycle of the Axolotl. WildAnimalsPedia. https://wildanimalspedia.com/the-fascinating-life-cycle-of-the-axolotl/

Maex, M., Van Bocxlaer, I., Mortier, A., Proost, P., & Bossuyt, F. (2016). Courtship pheromone use in a model urodele, the Mexican axolotl (Ambystoma mexicanum). Scientific Reports, 6(1). https://doi.org/10.1038/srep20184

Meet the Peter Pan of salamanders, the axolotl. (n.d.). Worldwildlife.org. https://www.worldwildlife.org/magazine/issues/summer-2021/articles/meet-the-peter-pan-of-salamanders-the-axolotl#:~:text=Axolotls%20were%20named%20after%20Xolotl,translated%20as%20%E2%80%9Cwater%20dog.%E2%80%9D

Mexican axolotl. (2014, March 1). National Geographic. https://kids.nationalgeographic.com/animals/amphibians/facts/mexican-axolotl

Michelle. (2022a, January 4). How to make A paper plate lion. Taming Little Monsters. https://taminglittlemonsters.com/paper-plate-lion/

Michelle. (2022b, September 2). Easy egg carton monkey craft for kids. Taming Little Monsters. https://taminglittlemonsters.com/egg-carton-monkey-craft-for-kids/

Michelle. (2022c, September 27). Easy craft stick monkey for kids. Taming Little Monsters. https://taminglittlemonsters.com/craft-stick-monkey/

Mike. (2023, April 27). Axolotl life cycle [stages, diagram, facts]. Amphibian Life. https://www.amphibianlife.com/axolotl-life-cycle-stages/

Morgan, A. (2023, June 1). What would happen if axolotls went extinct? Online Field Guide. https://www.online-field-guide.com/what-would-happen-if-axolotls-went-extinct/

naveenakhriya. (2023, June 27). The fascinating life cycle of an axolotl with pictures. Axolotl Expert. https://axolotlexpert.com/life-cycle-of-an-axolotl/

Nye, H. L. D., Cameron, J. A., Chernoff, E. A. G., & Stocum, D. L. (2003). Extending the table of stages of normal development of the axolotl: Limb development. Developmental Dynamics: An Official Publication of the American Association of Anatomists, 226(3), 555–560. https://doi.org/10.1002/dvdy.10237

OConnell, R. (2015, April 16). 11 fascinating axolotl facts. Mental Floss. https://www.mentalfloss.com/article/63130/11-awesome-axolotl-facts

Okafor, J. (2022, October 14). 15 cute axolotl facts and why are they endangered? TRVST. https://www.trvst.world/biodiversity/cute-axolotl-facts/

Raina, K. (2019, April 30). 12+ fun animal games and activities for kids. FirstCry Parenting. https://parenting.firstcry.com/articles/10-fun-animal-games-and-activities-for-kids/

Richard A. Griffiths, Ian G. Bride, Alejandro Meléndez, Jorge G. Álvarez-Romero, Fernando Arana. (2003). Researchgate.net. https://www.researchgate.net/publication/283712016_The_cons ervation_of_the_axolotl_Ambystoma_mexicanum_in_Xochimilc o_Mexico_City_a_specieshabitat_action_plan

See axolotls in the wild. (2016, October 10). National Geographic. https://www.nationalgeographic.com/animals/amphibians/facts/ axolotl

See axolotls in the wild. (2016, October 10). National Geographic. https://www.nationalgeographic.com/animals/amphibians/facts/ axolotl

Shaw, J. (n.d.). Why is biodiversity important? Conservation.org. https://www.conservation.org/blog/why-is-biodiversity-important

The amazing axolotl: A valuable model for regenerative medicine. (n.d.). Nih.gov. https://orip.nih.gov/about-orip/research-highlights/amazing-axolotl-valuable-model-regenerative-medicine

Vance, E., & Nature magazine. (n.d.). Biology's beloved amphibian--the axolotl--is racing toward extinction. Scientific American. https://www.scientificamerican.com/article/biologys-beloved-amphibian-the-axolotl-is-racing-toward-extinction1/

What is an Axolotl? The Ultimate Guide - SeaQuest ≥(◕ ᴗ ◕)≤. (2022, May 12). SeaQuest. https://visitseaquest.com/blog/seaquests-guide-to-axolotls/

Made in United States
Troutdale, OR
03/09/2024

18340055R00056